How to Become a 20-Something Millionaire

Tips on Realizing Your Dream of Retiring Young

By: Sandra Rodriguez

9781635019872

I0500166

PUBLISHERS NOTES

Disclaimer – Speedy Publishing LLC

Speedy Publishing LLC

40 E Main Street, Newark, Delaware, 19711

Contact Us: 1-888-248-4521

Website: http://www.speedypublishing.co

REPRINTED Paperback Edition: 9781635019872:

Manufactured in the United States of America

DEDICATION

This book is dedicated to my children, Nathan and Theodore. I will never regret my decision of fighting for you. You are such sweet blessings to my life. I could never imagine living without seeing your smiles.

TABLE OF CONTENTS

Chapter 1- What Every Young Entrepreneur Needs to Know but Books Left Out

Until now you have read some of the characteristics of entrepreneurship. "Practice makes perfect" is the motto about everything in life and especially if you are a business owner. Bookish knowledge can help you a lot to avoid mistakes but nothing beats the practical hands on experience of seeing what works for you. You have the right passion, the right business format and all the skills. But before making the leap of faith make sure you are ready in some other aspects as well.

From starting the business to make it run smoothly requires a lot of dedication and sacrifice. Which means young or old, personal life will take some hits. Family and friends must be supportive as they must know what it takes to start a business and its effect on your family life. Lot of you may choose to have a job in the initial days of starting a business; this means all your spare time has to go for running the business.

Entrepreneurship will take its toll on your health. Being lean and mean is great for business but that often means spending longer hours doing yourself what you would pay other people to do. Thus for surviving those 14+ hour work days, seven days a week you must be at the top of your physical and mental condition. Proper nutrition and a regular exercise regime will take care of your health. It's hard to enjoy the success lying down in the hospital bed. Know your strong points in business and hire others to do the other jobs.

Many owners think that they must be good at doing everything. This is surely not the case. Though at times knowing every aspect of the business is advantageous. Just in case anyone falls sick. From an entrepreneurial point of view having a team where you are the weakest link is not bad. Along with knowing your strong points you also must know your comfort zones.

Are you comfortable being the boss and having employees who are older than you? Dealing with the multiple personalities your employees possess? Handle money and take financial decisions? Getting into debt first for starting the business before seeing profits? Spare some years before you see enough profit to provide you a steady paycheck with? All these are just a few things you should keep in mind and keep a backup plan or two ready just in case you run into them down the road.

Sandra Rodriguez
Successful Entrepreneurs Need Ideas, Luck and Money

To become a successful entrepreneur you need good ideas, a little luck, money and lots of hard work. 90% of successful people fail, which means to gain something (profits, equity etc.) you must first lose something (your initial investment). Phat-farm is a multimillionaire company whose owner Russell Simmons lost 10 million dollars in the first five years. A lot of experience and resources is not required but to become a successful entrepreneur you need to have passion and persistence.

Turning everyday ideas into business is what makes an ordinary entrepreneur extraordinary. This talent or gift is what makes them unique. Most start with very limited resources and go ahead of their competitors through personal effort. The moves have to be fast and good decisions needs to be taken to gain share in the market and move forward for bigger competitors. They differ in age, sex and race but it's easy to spot an entrepreneur and their business. They might grow richer with their ideas but the startup point is to look for areas not being served and change the way things are done. A good idea is not the same as an ideal opportunity. Understanding the distinction will save your time, effort and money. The entrepreneur creates a vision and pushes the company through ups and downs towards fulfilling that vision.

Becoming an entrepreneur is at the same time scary, thrilling, worrisome, yet an exciting experience. But before you become one you have to understand the concept of entrepreneurship first. There are many types of entrepreneurs such as social, home based, virtual, traditional etc. The widely accepted definition of entrepreneurship would be to start up a new organization or take over an old one to respond to certain identified opportunities. You must be made aware that a large part of new businesses fail. The most successful people are they who are not afraid to experiment, and learn from their past mistakes and rectify to become successful. The difference between an entrepreneur and a small business owner is the process or method they want to inculcate for the expansion of the business.

Small business owners would want their business to be the way they are i.e. small and geographically bound only making a few millions in their entire lifespan. Entrepreneurial ventures look for earning millions in the first 3-5 years and expand internationally utilizing all opportunities. Other characteristics would be being focused, inclined towards innovation, and create new values to shake up the marketplace. In America small businesses provide maximum jobs whereas entrepreneurs provide most of the new jobs.

Attributes That Determine Success

Leadership qualities are not something you are born with and therefore needs to be acquired if you are an aspiring business person. The skills can be easily acquired if you keep in mind a few basic things that are necessary for any kind of leadership, be it in business or otherwise. The success of any business enterprise depends on how efficient the manager or the owner is in terms of building up a work culture that is healthy as well as productive.

Any leader should have a vision for the job that he is managing. It is important to have the right kind of vision for this is extremely crucial in holding together the various aspects of the job. A misplaced vision will not only lead the employees astray but also ruin the whole business. A clear vision will get you started and also help you see the work through in a successful way. A vision is something that the whole company works towards and it keeps them going until it is achieved.

Effective entrepreneurship will help the manager and his employees in realizing this vision. Ideas and opinions should be pooled in from all sides. This would make everyone feel a part of the whole enterprise. The manager should make sure that his employees are not merely skilled laborers who are there just to make money, but are committed to the vision of the company. The manager should inspire and motivate the employees to work towards a common goal. The business would thus become a means to achieving these ends. This does not mean that the focus should entirely be on the results and not on the work itself. Each step taken by the employees should be carefully analyzed and the employees should be given feedback on how the work is progressing. This would ensure expert quality as well as commendable results for the company.

The leader should create a healthy atmosphere in the work area that provides the employees with the space and freedom to think freely and apply his imagination in getting the work done. A rigid system of work would alienate the employees from each other and from the leader. This would jeopardize the whole system and affect the vision of the company. Any kind of business includes the target audience, which are the customers of the company. The leader should also focus on the customers by bringing out results that would reach out to a larger audience.

CHAPTER 2- HOW TO USE YOUR AGE TO YOUR ADVANTAGE

You are just a kid now, concentrate on studies. For business you need experience. Blah blah blah… People will have numerous reasons for why you shouldn't start a business, all out of good intentions only. But before you gulp down all that, think for a while about Bill Gates who left Harvard to start Microsoft, Michael Dell who left the University of Texas to start Dell, Milton Hershey who opened his first candy shop when he was 18, Fred Smith who, while attending Yale, received a "C" on his FedEx business plan and decided to start his business anyway, Steve Jobs who left Reed University to start Apple, William Hewlett and David Packard who started HP out of a garage after graduating from Stanford or the thousands of other young people who have started a business and been successful. What would have happened if they were convinced about these lame arguments and backed from their business plan??

We will have to live without a Dell, a Microsoft, an HP, a Hershey's, a FedEx or an Apple... oh! Horror horror!!! Best ways to tip the card in your favor: Adults expect less from young people and it can be used to your advantage. It's OK if you're not perfectly polished. It will take less effort to please clients and make a name for yourself with the media. There's little competition from other students, which makes your story more press-, scholarship-, competition-, client- and award-worthy. There are many nonprofit organizations and individuals that support youthful endeavors.

First on this list is your school, which probably has teachers who have contacts in the business community that can help you. Students often have income coming in from their parents. Even if it's not consistent, then it's at least something you know you can always look for. If you're venture fails when you're young, you definitely won't starve or lose your house.

The practical knowledge you learn from running your business can help your academic work and vice-versa. Some schools will allow you to earn academic credit from an independent study of your business. You can also base class projects on your business. Young people have a fresh perspective on the world. This perspective helps them to see many opportunities that were till now not been exploited. The founders of Microsoft, Dell, HP, Hershey's, Apple and Forex will vouch for you.

Strategic Thinking Is Possible Without Experience

Strategic thinking is as much science as art form. You need to use both the right and left side of your brain in order to truly excel, and this takes both confidence and practice. The following are some skills great strategists' possess and use daily: They envision great things and then use strategic thinking to make it real. Having both these abilities means that they can see a desirable future and evolve a strategy which focuses at the on the details and the big picture, in order to create it. Take time off from the daily hassles of a 9-5 job. All great strategists do this. Just go to a quiet place— preferably a weekend retreat, but a day or even an afternoon off, failing that—and sit with your thinking hat on. Try it.

Strategic thinking, as the name shows, isn't about making a quick buck; it's about seeing the big picture and planning for coming years. The immediate results might not be impressive, but in the long run, strategic thinking pays off. A reason for the perhaps-unimpressive immediate pay-off is that strategies, like masterpieces, take time to create, fine-tune and revise. All true strategists are entirely aware of everything happening around them. In all business concerns, there are bound to be clues, be they subtle or otherwise, that alert those who notice them of the possible directions in which the concern can be taken.

As great strategists absorb this information, it helps them better formulate their plans whenever inspiration strikes them, be it on a vacation, during a morning walk, or just after the first cup of espresso. Their ability to spot and create links holds them in good stead. Make sure your great idea isn't just a pipe-dream. All great thinkers should make sure that their idea is valid, that it'll stand up in a world full of problems and changes. You need to constantly revise and fine-tune your plans. Use experiences you've undergone to help you plan better. If a short-cut has worked before and saved you a lot of time and effort, don't hesitate to adapt it to a new plan. Don't depend just on yourself, no matter how good you think and/or know yourself to be. Use dependable colleagues to bounce your ideas off. In case of strategic thinking, 'two heads are better than one' is a truer adage than 'too many cooks spoil the broth'.

Repeatable Steps to Creating an Effective Business Plan for Starters

Before starting a small business first understand the need of the target market and then try to provide a suitable solution. These 7 steps are to be used by entrepreneurs who want to start a new venture or create a marketing plan for an existing successful set up. Most people talk about the greatness of their products or services. Instead you should regularly educate the target market and build a relationship of trust and credibility.

"Think marketing" is the mindset to be developed for your products and services. You have to market constantly. Do not fall for stop and go marketing. Some small businessmen start marketing during down seasons only. Having a successful marketing plan is essential for the venture. Profits and growth are directly proportional to effective marketing. If you are thinking where to start this 7 step guide will help you to understand the market and business.

Let's answer the following questions:

1. Who--- Who is your target market? Who is your ideal client? What is the research to be done for finding out more about the target market?

2. What--- What does your ideal client want? What does your product and services do for them? What problems of your customer are solved by your product? What solutions does your client require? What is your USP that makes you unique? What are industry trends? What will make your client react? What are you selling? (For e.g.: are you selling eyeglasses or vision?) What is your brand of product and services? What would be the price?

3. Where--- Where is your ideal client? Geographically where are they located? Where will you position yourself for their easy reach? Where will they get you marketing messages from? Will you go through personal conversations, hold seminars or write a blog, newsletter or article?

4. When--- How frequent will you be with your marketing messages? When are your clients most likely to purchase?

5. Why--- Why are you in business? Why will customers come to you? Why should they not go to your competitors and choose your products?

6. How--- How does your customer purchase? How will you reach out to potential clienteles? How are you going to communicate your marketing strategies? How will you provide information to your customers to make their buying decision?

7. Marketing mindset--- Try to master a marketing mindset and your small business will move towards profits and success.

CHAPTER 3- SECRETS, MISTAKES AND MYTHS WHEN STARTING A BUSINESS

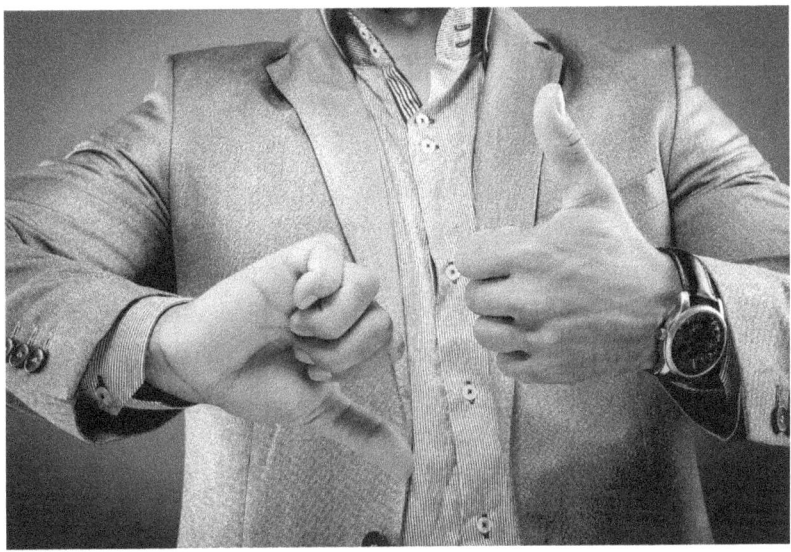

The starting up of a business brings upon some significant changes in the business owner's life:

1) The permanent financial freedom,

2) Flexibility of schedule,

3) Satisfaction of making one's life fulfilled- irrespective of making the business grow into a mammoth structure or just keep doing what you like to do and earn your living.

Beside the excitement of new ventures arrive the challenge of wearing too many hats- strategic planning, marketing, sales, production, customer support, accounting and financing. Even if the business is small the tasks are huge. Whatever might be the field, the main factors of a successful venture remains the same-

How to Become a 20-Something Millionaire
1) A good idea,

2) An effective marketing plan that is not hugely expensive,

3) Efficient operation.

Ideas

A proper business idea is crucial for the success of the venture. Firstly you must be passionate about the area of work. Secondly you must possess enough knowledge, talent and experience to stick on. Finally, choose a business that'll yield small and steady income without heavy investment. This will eventually support you and your family. Some ideas that can be considered are- freelance writing, online marketing, web design, book keeping etc.

Promotion

Basic tool of marketing your product and services would be distributing business cards. You can design the card yourself by using different business card templates but it would be wiser to spend some money and let a professional do it. As little as 20$ will get you 500 cards. Color cards are a bit more expensive.

Next step is to build a website which will allow the prospects to view the information 24 hrs. 365 days. Around 50$ is the cost for web holding per year. Another 80$ more would get you two simple web pages. If the internet prospects look good, then spend $50 on pay-per-click (PPC) online ads. $50 on PPC will bring you more customers and also generate revenue.

Operation Efficiency

Running the business (marketing, sale, production etc.) takes away all the time for small business owners. They don't have time (or knowledge) on strategizing the expansion of the business. The result is that they either remain a small venture or get wiped out if there's a drastic change in the market. Operation efficiency is even more required in smaller ventures than in established farms.

Some methods of improving operation efficiency-

1) Streamline business process,

2) Utilize productivity software,

3) Outsourcing and etc.

Something like- hiring an accountant for tax returns and bookkeeping, a collection agency for debt collection etc. should be done. Always spend time in expanding your business.

Common Mistakes to Avoid

An economy primarily consists of producers and consumers, and they engage in what is known as transaction. An economic transaction would be the transfer of goods and services from the producers to the consumers in exchange for money. Creation of goods involves various activities. These activities can be collectively known as a business, or a firm. Starting a business is neither easy nor quick. Here are a few essentials required to do the same.

What to Produce?

There are many goods that an economy consists of. Hence, the producer must decide on which of these to produce. Looking out for one's own profit cannot be the only criteria. Resources are scarce, and they should be used optimally and towards the societal welfare.

How to Produce?

There can be many methods of producing one commodity. Hence, the producer should opt for that process which exploits the resources fully at minimal cost.

How Much to Produce?

An excess of supply will lower the price and the producers will eventually incur a loss. Hence, produce to cater to the market demand.

•Capital to start a business

One needs to have enough investment power. If a producer does not have the required capital he can take loans from financial institutions, or enter into partnership with other investors to get collective investment support.

•Market Study.

It is not enough to have the money to set up a business. One needs to understand the consumption patter of the market. Even if the product has high selling probability, it should be marketed in a way that it grabs the buyer's attention. Otherwise, consumers might not be fully aware of the product details.

•Scale of production

Normally, a business cannot reach the optimal production level in the short run. This is due to the fixed inputs of production that cannot be changed according to need. These inputs give rise to fixed costs which cut into the producer's revenue. However, with time as the business reaches a considerable scale, these fixed inputs disappear and only the variable ones remain, i.e. the producer faces only variable cost.

•Delegation of activities

No business can sustain on the basis of single showmanship. There are too many activities involved. Therefore, it is cheaper, more efficient and necessary to delegate duties to the individuals specializing in those fields. Hence, violation of any of the above guidelines is a mistake through which the business suffers.

Never Believe in Myths

There are a lot of myths about being an entrepreneur; most spawned by the media. While some these are true, others are patently false.

The following are the top five myths:

•Myth #1: Entrepreneurs want money. Period.

A lot of people think entrepreneurs are in it solely for the money. This is true to an extent —fear of poverty, or simply financial insecurity, might well goad anyone to greater heights, and there are some who do it for the cash, but for most people, money is not the be-all and end-all. A lot of entrepreneurs have ego and/or emotion as their primary motives, many don't maintain the lavish lifestyles expected of them, and most consider money as a way of keeping score.

•Myth #2: My gain, your loss.

People often refer to success in business at the cost of someone else. What they mean, obviously, is that if an entrepreneur is winning, someone somewhere has paid the price. This makes it seem like there has to be a winning and a losing side in every business deal. This is sometimes called the 'zero-sum game'. In actual fact, entrepreneurs are creative thinkers. Rather than play for a 'zero-sum' result, and contrary to popular supposition, they often try to work out a compromise that means everybody leaves the table satisfied.

•Myth #3: The greater the risk, the greater the reward.

A lot of young entrepreneurs, having heard this, accept it as gospel truth. A relationship between risk and reward is complicated and in no way reducible to a simple statement. Risks in business don't equalize jumping off a cliff in the dark: knowledge, experience, wisdom hard work and perseverance modify both the 'risk' and the 'reward'.

•Myth #4: Entrepreneurs get rich fast.

The rise of 'dotcom millionaires' definitely makes it seem like entrepreneurs make a quick buck, but you should remember nothing is as easy as it seems. You may think that entrepreneurs get extremely rich extremely fast, but a lot of hard work goes into developing the ideas/products that make them rich.

•Myth #5: A good business plan is the entrepreneur's critical roadmap to success.

This has more truth than most of the other myths, as you're unlikely to be given loans without a solid business plan. However, a loan does not in any way equal good money. Business plans are guidelines, yes, but to succeed, you need a lot more.

CHAPTER 4- HOW THE YOUNG CAN BE SUCCESSFUL

Age is No Excuse for Ethics in Business

"Honesty is the best policy", a phrase that is valid not only in one's daily lives, but also in business ethics. Ethics are very important to all business people. Yet, many neglect ethics as an important concept that has a major impact upon a person's success as an entrepreneur and investor. Business, after all, involves dealing with money, either one's own or borrowed. It also involves building successful money based relationships with clients and customers. Such relationships must be built on trust – and having ethical foundations are imperative to the building of trust. Therefore ethics constitute the cornerstone of success in business.

It is important to realize that ethics is important irrespective of the size of the business. Whether your business enterprise is large or small, whether your customers are many or few, the relevance of adhering to high ethical standards is the same. You see, ethics in business is closely linked to the moral value chain that intertwines through all its operations. Moral value impinges on every single customer. There can be no exceptions irrespective of whether your customers are 10 or 10,000 in number or more. Ethics apply to each of them.

As a discipline, ethics in business can be either applied or theoretical. Or to express it differently, it can be either pragmatic or philosophical. The former evolves, typically, into the do's and don'ts that act as guidelines to achieving ethical behavior. The latter studies involve probing the whys and wherefores of ethics in business. It also examines the issue of defining ethics. It promotes high standards, draws up a code and helps the entrepreneur self-evaluate his own personal ethical standard.

This standard in turn helps the business enunciate the norms of ethical behavior of its employees. An honest business employs only honest professionals. This must be clearly understood down the line. In most successful business organizations high ethical standards are compulsory. An employee bribing somebody, even to further his employer's interests, is likely to be dismissed. Many multinationals refuse to conduct business in countries where bribes are commonly given and taken. These are examples of the applied side of ethics in business.

A final point: In some factors there can be no compromises in ethics irrespective of profit or loss considerations. For instance, under no circumstances should a business break the laws of the country where's it's in business whether it likes these laws or not.

Effective Communication Is Always Used

Even if you have brilliant ideas, they're worthless unless you share them. So, being able to communicate effectively is as important as being able to come up with great ideas. However, not everyone is good at communication, and they need practice to be capable of it. Suppose a situation arises when, due to external reasons, you need to immediately double your company's output. But your managers are unable to get the work done by the employees, who are unwilling to go that extra mile for the company. This results in loss of both money and reputation for the company. So, what's the problem? It's not that you're not paying the employees, nor are they deprived of other benefits. So the real problem here is the lack of communication between employer and employee.

It is often forgotten that internal communication is an integral part of business communication strategy. The entire focus being on external communication, the firm and its managers busily paint rosy pictures for customers. This leads to a strong marketing side, certainly, but rather weakens operational strategy. Another problem cause by miscommunication and/or lack of communication is the growth of the negative-grapevine. This unofficial channel of communication can lead to disaffection, causing profits to decrease.

To ensure growth, you need to have channels of both internal and external communication. The whole communication system should be of one piece and purpose. No loose talk can be permitted. Whatever is communicated, whether to the customers or the employees, must be carefully crafted in order to attain the goals that have been set.

If you focus on your target segment's needs, you are likely to be able to set up an effective communication strategy. They care about your goals, but only as far as they benefit from it. So identify with their needs and communicate your goals in terms they empathize with. If you welcome suggestions and encourage feedback, your employees get a chance to constructively put forward their suggestions, but this will also suppress the grapevine and allow them to feel involved.

When you receive the feedback or suggestions, react in a positive way. Assure your employees that their complaints are being noted and positive actions shall be taken. Make sure your message isn't lost in a maze of jargon and can be understood by your target audience. To sum up, to achieve your goals, you must communicate your ideas clearly.

A Good Business Owner Manages Time Well

Time management is considered to be the art which teaches you the diverse techniques to increase your effectiveness and complete pending work. It is important to be able to control and manage time in your personal life, but in case of your business, it is critical and necessary in order to achieve success.

Time management software helps small business owners to manage and control time effectively by using electronic calendars and planners. The 'to do list' is proven to be an effective tool in time management. Scheduling actions, however, is also time consuming, thus, it is an essential need to use software. Success is a result of planning your goals as well as your time, implementing routines and scheduling tasks.

Time management software can enforce the employee's flow of work and production activities by using written or electronic reminders or the 'to do list' software. It is a must for small business owners to plan, prepare, prioritize and control their activities along with the activities of other members of the team, and also set the goals towards the success of the business. This is actually an easy task once you have the adequate time management software.

Many of these software products include planning short and long term goals, data analysis, future predictions, and performance graphics. These are features that are not available in the basic to do list software. Do not under estimate the importance of the 'to do list' software when planning your business activities or setting your goals. Time management is extremely important for a small business. Thus, time management gurus are common these days who give out advice on how to set about managing your time. They are best known as time managers, who after reading your business plan; prioritize activities for work teams on a daily basis.

With the help of time management software, they can provide the business owners with the detailed reports of daily activity trends, allowing the owners to rectify values, activities and priorities. Time managers are also the common name given to time management software and various time management solutions available in the market today for small businesses. These range from the classic paper books, to diverse 'to do list' software, organizers, reminders, calendars and planners among many other things.

Chapter 5- Taking Baby Steps toward Business Success

How Much Should Your Capital Be?

Startup costs pose problems for all of us. They are instrumental into getting one into a fix and so measuring your stakes is very important. So here are ten beneficial tips on how to estimate your business startup costs.

1. First and foremost you need to think carefully and include the costs of all the various things you need in the estimated startup costs for your business. Always remember, that this amount is

different from the basic amount cost required for you and the company to survive for the year. Beside this, there are various other things that need money and that include advertisements, chairs and office supplies, inventory, cash registers, and service supplies. The startup cost must also have provision for any other item that you may have forgotten.

2. Don't take bank loans unless it is absolutely necessary. And even if you do ensure that you can afford the interest that the bank is going to charge. Also enquire after the interest rates; you wouldn't want it to be too high.

3. Take into account your household expenses during the period that is the starting time for your business. Make sure you have adequate cash to cover the amount or the credentials to acquire a loan that'll cover the amount.

4. You must be able to judge the amount of money that is required for your business to survive its first year. You also need to be prepared for any other sporadic expenses that might occur once in a while during that year.

5. Organize yourself so that you are ready for any extra additional costs that might come up intermittently throughout the year.

6. You need to take into consideration the expenses on food for the entire year. Your budget should leave sufficient money for food and other basic expenses. This will cushion you from risks during the first year of business.

7. Your company requires that credentials that'll secure a loan in case your money runs out sometime during the year. It is advisable that you get a loan only if you can generate enough

sales to pay the loan back. If your business is not doing very well during the first year then you might want to shut it down.

8. The salary that you have to pay to your employees, that is, if you have employees, is another thing that has to be kept in mind. That includes business insurance, any health insurance, and of course workers' payments. You also have to pay an extra fee to the city for any part time and full time employees you have working for your company.

9. You may have to take tests to get certified depending on the nature of the business that you are starting. These tests cost money. Moreover you have to be aware of any other rules and regulations that your type of business entails.

10. You can always sell some personal belongings to get some extra money in case you don't have enough. But ensure that your business offers sufficient security for selling these items. The last thing you want is end up broke having lost your company and also all your expensive belongings because you sold them to have enough money to start the company.

Where Will You Get the Money From?

Successful businessmen and women wanting to invest their capital in struggling businesses or startup franchises are called Business Angels. In return for the investment, they usually want convertible debt or ownership equity. In order to get a good return on their investment, they plan to use their expertise to turn the businesses into successes. Because of their experience, Business Angels are very careful about who they invest in. Their plan of action involves investing when the shares are cheap, working with the company, building it up and then selling the mature company after a few years to other stockbrokers or to the original owner.

Dragons Den is a popular program that has investors waiting to invest in a business. As the owner of a business, it is important to have a great sales pitch and to prepare in advance. It helps to have a clear business strategy. The dragons are usually good at noticing if the target audience and market has not been researched adequately. In order to impress the dragons, it is important to have accurate sales projections – they want facts as answers to their questions, not lies. They will usually not invest in a high-risk business if they believe it won't work. They are experts in their field, so their advice about business ideas is very valuable, and should be heeded.

Confidence is very important. Voice, posture and attitude are dead giveaways when it comes to confidence, so it helps to have these areas covered when convincing potential investors. Questions should be prepared for: thinking about what the investors might ask is a good strategy. Questions about potential profits and company income are natural, so they key is to think differently. Areas of the business that make it unique and different from others should be highlighted in order to eliminate competition.

Commitment is another vital factor. Business angels like to see committed workers. They are usually impressed if the business venture includes some of the starter's own capital. However, if thousands of pounds have already been invested in the business and it's still not making any money, they will be wary.

Business Angels nowadays are very easy to find, thanks to the Internet. There are hundreds of sites dedicated to finding the right investor for a business. Angel groups or angel networks also exist. Therefore, starting a business has never been easier – investment is a hand's throw away!

How Do You Want Your Business Remembered?

Attaching an identifiable brand to your business is very important to ensure success for your business. The term Branding is a conglomeration of numerous functions that must be undertaken to ensure success for the business. Branding initiates subsequent actions in diverse zones, like:

1. Increasing perception and visibility of business name and logo.

2. Formulating a company name that can immediately inspire public faith.

3. Identifying and carefully nurturing the potential consumer profile.

Branding, including the company name and logo, is not a tangible asset of a business, unlike physical assets like resources and institutions, and is only useful in increasing the goodwill of the business, and accentuating the reputation and identity of the business. Careful and cautious planning must go into branding, before it is implemented for profit maximizing. Identifying and isolating attracting consumer base with specific incentives & comprehension of their requirements are to be ensured before branding is undertaken.

Some very essential steps to secure and devise a successful Brand for the business:

Consistency in Advertisements:

Advertising your brand involves showcasing and emphasizing the unique points of the brand, which the competitors lack. These points are to be repeatedly stressed and advertised, so that it creates a recall value within its customer base. The public is to be absolutely showered with these advertisements so that they are reminded of these brands regularly.

Consumer Service:

Human resource is a very vital ingredient for the success of any business, and so, proper recruitment of sales staff is essential. They are to be certain about their position in the process of brand building. Every customer needs to be respected and understood, and being inattentive or unmindful of even a single customer can mean massive losses for the business. Uncooperative staff should be sacked, because favorable response from a customer helps attract ten more.

How Does the Public Perceive Your Brand?

The treatment of a single customer can spread very fast on word of the mouth, and negative publicity jeopardizes your business. While brand promotion, illegitimate and false promises are not to be made. The purchasing and billing process is to be simplified to ensure customer convenience. Prior commitments are to be respected, punctually, to increase goodwill of the brand.

Use of Technology

The denial of the impact of internet in business promotion and marketing would be improper. Internet queries from customers must be satisfactorily answered. The business must also be regularly updated and implemented with advanced technologies.

CHAPTER 6- HOW TO USE THE INTERNET AS STRATEGY FOR MARKETING

An essential component of effective Internet marketing is managing your reputation and your company's reputation online. Consumers often engage in Internet research before choosing a product or service as well as the provider of that product or service.

It is quite common for a consumer to research your company name, your name and your URL before making a final decision as to whether or not to use your company. This fact makes it essential that you engage in effective reputation management.

Managing What the Internet Is Saying About You

You have to know what is being said about you (both positive and negative) in order to manage your reputation. It is impossible for you to check all the different websites that people post comments and reviews on. Luckily for you, you can set up a Google alert to notify you anytime your name, business' name or URL appear somewhere on the net. Go to http://www.google.com/alerts to set them up.

How to Handle Negative Postings

Negative postings will appear from time to time about you or your business. You should address them head-on but never get personal with the person who posted the comment. You should address your company's shortcomings and mention how you plan to make things better in the future.

You should let people know that you take customer service seriously. You can offer to help the customer receive some type of satisfaction if at all possible. The key is to show people that your company listens and actually cares.

If you get into a battle of jabs and insults you will always lose. Do not get baited into such a situation.

Bury Bad Links with Good Ones

You want to make sure you distribute positive information about you and your company as often as possible. Make sure the information is honest and pertinent. The information you post on the Internet can be about charitable donations, new product launches, awards won, etc. The key is you want this information to appear in the search results above the negative postings.

Frequent positive postings are the best way to combat negative publicity. Online press releases, articles, social media sites and pages, forum postings and blog postings focused on your name and your company's name will go a long way towards helping manage your reputation online.

Your Internet marketing strategy must include allocating resources towards reputation management for you and your company.

Identifying Buying Cycles

Internet marketing is a powerful way to grow your business. Your insight into your target market is a key component to succeeding online. If you know the buying cycle of your target market you will be able to effectively market to them at all stages of it.

Beginning of Buying Cycle

Every industry will have buyers that start their buying cycle with some basic research about the products or services they are interested in. By doing some keyword research you can identify these early-stage buyers and capture their attention before your competitors do. Here are the types of search terms they will use:

• Printer reviews

• Best DVD players

• Luxury sedan comparisons

The terms they use when searching will clearly identify the fact that they are in the information gathering process. Provide them the information they want on your site and via e-mail so you can follow-up market to them.

Mid Stages of Buying Cycle

As consumers progress in the buying cycle they will start narrowing their online searches. For example they may use terms like:

• Color laser printer

• Sony DVD players

• Lexus models

At this stage they have narrowed in on what they want but have not necessarily made a final selection. This is an Important stage in the buying cycle where you need to give consumers information that will push them towards purchasing.

Stages of Buying Cycle

This is the stage that most people focus on. The final stage of the buying cycle is when a consumer is ready to buy. The types of search terms at this point are:

• Epson Stylus 900

• Sony HD-9180

• Lexus LS 450

The consumer identified what they want to buy and are now looking for where to buy it. This is when they need to know why they should buy it from you. You want to focus on service, price and reputation. If you focus your Internet marketing efforts only on the end stages of the process you will lose the opportunity to capture the interest of and loyalty of potential customers in the early stages. Take the time to give consumers at the earlier stages of the buying cycle the information they want and they will reward you with consumer confidence and loyalty.

All stages of the buying cycle should be part of your Internet marketing strategy.

Professional Appearance

The Internet has billions of web pages all competing for the interest of web users. Within any given industry there can be thousands or millions of websites that can be found. Once they are found your site visitors will make a snap decision as to whether or not they want to continue viewing your website.

The Initial Impression

The immediate impression someone gets of your website will determine whether or not they stay on your site or hit the "back" button. It is important that your site be easy on the eyes, easy to navigate and clear in its purpose.

Skip the flash introductions that people get frustrated waiting for. Though they will impress a handful of people, most people will ignore them and resent having to wait for them to load. Have a clean and clear landing page and you will be able to capture the interest of more people.

Make sure it takes less than 1-second for someone visiting your site to know what you are about. If you sell watches make sure there are watches on the landing page. If you are a lawyer make sure your landing page says where you practice and the type of law your practice. You have less than 2-seconds to make an impression so make it count.

Contact Information

Contact information is important. If you have a website there is no reason to use Gmail, Yahoo, AOL or other similar email addresses. Have an email address set for your specific domain. People will question the credibility of a website that uses this type of email address.

When contacting clients or potential clients make sure your email address is from your domain and is professionally written. You will lose credibility if your email is poorly written or comes from a Yahoo, Gmail, Hotmail or other type of account.

Have a phone number on your website even if it is for a virtual phone system that takes a message or forwards the calls to your home or cell phone. Consumers want to see phone numbers on websites.

Quality of Content

The quality of your website content is vital. Make sure it is well written, error-free, clear and concise. Your failure on any one of these three points will make you lose credibility in the eyes of your target market.

Consider the above factors and make sure your site appears professional to your target market.

Basics of Link Building

A component to succeeding online is to have a network of websites that link to you. This will help you generate traffic and rank better in search results. Before you start link building you need to know the different methods as well as their pros and cons.

Manual Link Building

There are a number of different ways to link build. The most established way is requesting a link from a website owner or webmaster. You want to find websites that are on the same or similar topic as yours and ask them for a link to your website (you may want to offer one to them in exchange).

You need to send an e-mail to the contact person you find on the website and make the request. Chances are you will need to follow up more than once before getting a response. If you do not get a response after 5 or 6 requests you may be better off moving on.

The pro of this type of link building is that it is considered a fairly ethical practice. The con of this type of link build is that it is very labor intensive.

Buying Links

As you can imagine, there have been some very industrious people who saw an opportunity to make money and have created networks where people can buy links on other people's websites and sell links on their site.

In a matter of minutes you can buy links to your website from websites on a similar topic (the only value in link building is if you get links from sites on a similar topic).

The major pro with this type of link building is that it is fast. The major con is that Google specifically forbids it and will penalize or ban any website caught doing it.

Links through Content Distribution

Distributing articles and press releases is a great way to build links to your website. If you write (or have written) articles and press releases that are relevant you can build a considerable network of links into your site. The better the articles and press releases are the better the results will be.

The major pro for this type of link building is that it is effective and ethical. The major con is that if you are not a good writer you will need to find one.

Importance of Landing Pages

Landing pages are an essential part of a successful Internet marketing plan. It is quite common for a website to have different landing pages with marketing efforts focused on driving specific traffic to specific landing pages.

Multiple Pages

Most websites sell a variety of products or at the very least different models. For example, a fashion website may sell pants, shoes, shirts, skirts, blouses, etc. A website that sells watches may sell gold watches, silver watches, divers' watchers, etc.

You want to bring consumers to a specific page on your site. Someone looking for a leather skirt does not want to land on a web page that does not immediately show them that you sell leather skirts. Someone looking for a gold watch wants to land on a page that makes it clear you sell gold watches.

In short you need to give people what they want from the very first second they arrive on your website.

Content and Images

Try to get in the mindset of your target market and make sure your landing pages speak directly to that target audience. If your primary target market is females 18 – 24, make sure all images appeal to girls ages 18 to 24. If your target market is men and women 40 – 55 years old, make sure your images appeal to that target market.

In addition to your images appealing to your target market you want to make sure the content appeals to them as well. Your target market must feel comfortable with your site in order to build consumer confidence and loyalty.

Call to Action

Every landing page must include a call to action. A call to action can be to click on a link to learn more, add something to a shopping cart, leave their e-mail address, etc. You must identify what action you want the website visitor to take and make sure it is easy for them to take it.

Everything you want a consumer to do should be 1 to 2 clicks away at most. If they need to navigate through too many pages there is a good chance you will lose their interest before you got them to the final call to action.

The bottom line is to make sure you have landing pages that appeal to all segments of your target market and you should see an increase in your conversion rates.

CHAPTER 7- AFFILIATE MARKETING – WHERE EVERY YOUNG ENTREPRENEUR STARTS

Affiliate marketing is a way of making money online. It's really a simple concept. When you are an affiliate marketer, you promote a product, service, or site for a business, and you as a publisher get rewarded for doing so.

In most cases, you find products related to your niche and offer them on your website or blog. You promote the products and post a link on your site where they can purchase the products. Then, when someone follows that link to buy something, you earn a commission. The commissions can be either a percentage of the sale or a fixed amount. You've seen links to other sites when you've read other people's blogs. These links make the blogger money.

For example: I write a book about affiliate marketing. Your blog is centered on tips to make money online. You actually promote and sell the book from your site. You get a percentage of the sale. It's like being paid an advertising or marketing fee. You may also sell other products that are related to your site.

For example: You blog about cooking and recipes. There are endless numbers of cooking related appliances or utensils you could sell from your site to make it easier for them to prepare those recipes. In other cases, you might earn an amount when someone follows the link and take some kind of action such as: sign up for something with their email address or complete a survey with their name and address.

Your earnings are usually tracked by using a link that has a code embedded in it. This link is only used by you. They may also be tracked when the advertiser gives you a coupon code. You've probably followed a link from another site at one time or another online. You've also probably bought something where you enter a code. When customers do this, you make money without doing a thing. They do the work for you.

There are a few factors that help make your affiliate marketing successful.

They include:

• The amount of traffic you have. The higher the traffic, the greater your earning potential will be.

• The quality of the products you recommend. Recommending junk products can really hurt you, so you want to make sure what you recommend will be a value to your readers.

• The amount of trust your readers have in you. If you have established trust, your readers are more likely to click on the link.

Publishers like affiliate marketing for the obvious reason...you get paid while someone else does the work. You may be in bed asleep and still be earning money. If you find a product that is relevant to your niche, your earnings can be good if you have a large following. You may be wondering why an advertiser would pay people for advertising in this manner. It's a matter of cost. They may pay a lot of money for an advertising campaign that doesn't pay off.

With affiliate marketing, however, they only pay when the advertising pays off. If they have a network of affiliates they may make less per sale, but overall, their sales will increase. If you have a good level of trust with the people who read your blog, they will trust that you wouldn't recommend something they wouldn't like. This will cause them to at least look at what you're recommending. With the right sales pitch online, you can make it something they "must" have. If they purchase something from you and it is a good product that they like, they're more apt to buy another. They'll also pass on where they got it. That will lead more traffic to your site and increase your sales.

Why Do Affiliate Marketing?

If you're looking for a way to make money online, you should consider affiliate marketing. There are numerous benefits to becoming an affiliate.

These include:

• There's no production cost

If you wanted to set up a business selling products online you'd have to buy, ship, and store the products. It can be costly. If you have an affiliate program, production cost isn't an issue. The merchant has already paid for the development of the product.

•The set-up cost is low

You probably already have a desk, an internet connection, and a computer. That's all you need to get started.

•There are no fees or licenses to pay

Affiliate programs are usually free to join. Your geographic market reach is as big as your ability to promote your site. The internet is a worldwide marketplace. You can take advantage of this market.

•You can sell almost anything

There are a few blog sites that probably wouldn't be able to find a product to promote that is related to their niche, but they are limited. Almost everything you can think of is sold online. There are thousands of affiliate programs, so it is easy to find products related to your current site or the site you are planning to set up.

•You don't have to handle any sales to make money from them

You have no inventory, no order processing, and no shipping to deal with. You are making money from sales by promoting the products, not having taken care of the actual sales process.

•You can work from home

If you've ever had a long commute to work, you can really appreciate the ability to work from home. It's also a great way to get to spend more time with your family. You won't have the normal work expenses like gas, buying lunch, wardrobe, etc. You can work from home in the comfort of your pajamas if you want.

•If you have your computer with you, you can work from anywhere in the world

Have you ever wanted to travel, but taking off from work isn't an option? If so, affiliate marketing is perfect. You take your office with you. You wouldn't have to spend more than a few hours a day working, and you could visit anywhere you wanted and still be able to work.

•There is a minimal level of risk

If you try to sell a product and it isn't making you any money, you just stop selling it and try something else. All you have to do is take down your links and promote another product. It's that simple. You don't have to worry about being stuck in a long-term contract that binds you to promote a product that doesn't sell.

•There is potential for high income

With your own affiliate business online, your potential for income is only limited by your efforts. Granted, not everyone makes a lot of money.

You have to be willing to put forth the effort to find, set up, and promote the products. If you promote your products well and build traffic to your site, you can have a successful affiliate business.

How Does It Work?

People who want to make money online usually struggle with creating a website, ads, sales and closing scripts. They also have their own merchant account services. A few people may actually enjoy going through that process, but for those who don't have the time, energy, or desire to put forth that much energy, affiliate marketing is ideal. If you want to make money online using affiliate marketing, you don't have to worry about the setup.

The company usually provides you with information about the product and product reviews or testimonials that you can use, however, most people prefer to write their own personal product reviews. Your payment gateway is already set up by the business. You don't have to worry about handling the money or dealing with refunds.

Here are a few different areas of affiliate marketing and how it works in these areas:

1. What You Offer

All you need to do is use a search engine like Google, and you can find a list of affiliate programs. A broad search will let you know every program out there. You may want to only be an affiliate for products in your niche.

If so, then just search for the niche you're interested in such as:

• Electronics Affiliate Programs

• Cosmetic Affiliate Programs

• Food Preparation

Affiliate Programs, whatever niche you want, can probably be found by simple searching for it. You may want to look at some of the affiliate resources that are popular like Clickbank.com or Amazon.com. There will be a distributor form. It has the terms and conditions that tell you how you're allowed to sell their products and what the commission is.

Here are a few good tips to remember when you're selecting a product:

1. First, you have either have a website or blog to make decent earnings. If you don't at least have a blog, you should begin one today. Focus it on topics that you are interested in and know a lot about. With each Clickbank product there are some statistics mentioned, let me explain them:

2. Select products that are related to the niche of your website/blog.

3. Find items where you'll end up making at least $20 per sale.

4. A good gravity range for selecting products is a range of 50- 120.

5. There are some products out there that offer at least 75% commission. It is good to select those where you'll make at least 50%.

6. Find products with good landing pages. If you're not satisfied with the way the website looks for the product you're promoting, it will probably be hard for you to convince your audience to buy those products. Look for well-written sales copy.

7. The best way to sell the products you promote is to find those products that help your readers solve a problem.

2.Cost

It is usually free to sign up to be an affiliate. Some programs require a small monthly or annual fee. This helps the business their website, training, overhead, and use of their payment processors. Some vendors will require that the affiliate purchase the product in order to make the biggest commission. They feel you should have the product and use it so you'll be prepared to give it a better recommendation based on your first-hand experience working with the product.

3. Earning commissions

The percentage of commission will vary depending on the vendor's terms and the vendor's conditions. There isn't a set commission, and the amount of commission can vary greatly. The commission you receive is based on these things:

• Commission structure of the product you wish to sell

• The number of people who purchase the product—this will depend on how you advertise it and how well you connect with the audience you are targeting

• Whether or not the affiliate program is a program that is leveraged

It is practically impossible to truly determine how much you will make. The variables are just too great. It really depends on you.

4. Receiving commissions

Every vendor has their own method of paying commissions. There are vendors that will pay you on a regular basis no matter how little or how much you earn. Others, however, will not pay you until you reach a minimum threshold. They can pay you in different intervals such as: Instantly, weekly, bimonthly, monthly, or quarterly. The types of payment you receive can vary as well. You can be paid by using ways such as: A check in the mail, PayPal, direct deposit, Federal Express, or pay through a debit card.

5. Tracking sales

You will be assigned your own ID. It will be built into your website URL when you sign up and are approved to be an affiliate. It works like this. Let's say you find a company named www.letsgodecocrazy.com. You find the site and sign as an affiliate for their product. They will ask you for a user name. You select "zigzag." The username can be built into your URL as a way to advertise. Sometimes the company assigns you something different. Sometimes it just looks like a very long line of numbers, letters, and characters. Whatever is used, that's the URL you need to use to send your traffic to. When they buy by clicking on your link, you get the agreed upon commission.

6. Sign up process

Research and find an affiliate that right for you. When you find it, go to their website. Look for something like, "Affiliates," "Join Affiliate Program," or "Partners Program." Carefully read their terms and conditions. View all the products they offer. You want to make sure they are what you're looking for. If you clearly understand what you can and can't do when selling the product and you feel the commission rate is sufficient, sign up. They should direct you to a form to fill out online. If you don't find an affiliate application, you can either call them or email them and request one. They will want to know your name, address, phone, email, and if they give you a choice, how you want to be paid. Be prepared to give them your Social Security number. This is for tax purposes, and you will receive a 1099at the end of the year. Some request it at the time of the application and others hold your earnings until they receive it. If you don't provide it within the time frame requested, however, you will forfeit any earnings you've made.

7. Marketing

There are many different ways you can market your product/service online. Sometimes, it will depend on what the product or service is. It will also depend on you and where your talents and preferences lie. Here are a few of them:

• Blogging

If you like to write, you may want to write a blog post that tells what the benefit of your product/service is. You can use your unique URL and link it to your affiliate website.

• Videos

If you don't like to write, perhaps making a video would work better for you. You can tell your viewers about the benefits of your product. Then, just like the blog, you link it using your URL.

• Articles

You can write and submit articles. When you submit the articles to directories, you include the benefits of the product/service. Always remember to link it to the affiliate with your own URL.

• Social Media

The benefits of social media are endless. If you don't have a social media page of some kind, such as Facebook, Twitter, or LinkedIn, you need to have at least one. You can write a blog or make a note why you're recommending this particular product/service and post your link on your wall.

• Solo Ads

You can find a list that is a good fit for your product/service with an audience that will be interested in it and have solo ads for that product

Chapter 8- Finding Potential Customers Online Traffic

Internet marketing was dramatically changed with the introduction of social media sites including Facebook, Myspace and Twitter. Since Twitter was first launched people have wondered how they should use it as part of their Internet marketing plan.

The Basics of Twitter

Twitter allows you to post to your followers messages of up 140 characters in length. You may be wondering how much you can say in only 140 characters. Join the club. Everyone wonders that until they get the hang of it and you will. Follow a few simple rules and you will do just fine on Twitter.

What to Tweet

It is important that your tweets be more than a constant barrage of promotional messages. You will quickly lose your followers. The general rule to follow is the 80-20 rule. 80% of your tweets should be either useful or entertaining to your followers. The other 20% of your tweets can be direct promotions of your products and services.

An effective Internet marketing plan using Twitter should include humor. Humor can help you maintain long-term online relationships with your followers. People appreciate humor even if you are just providing links to humor sites, video clips, etc.

Promotional Tweets

What you say in the 140 characters of your promotional tweets is important. If you do it properly you should be able to bring targeted traffic to your website. Your promotional tweets must entice your followers to click on your accompanying link to read more about the promotion. Do not try to close a sale in 140 characters. Get them to your website. That is your sole goal.

Grab your followers' attention quickly with a catchy line. Use questions (Do you want to save a bundle on a gift for Mom?), or exclamations (A sale so HUGE you won't believe it!). The key is grabbing their attention and making them want more information.

How often do I Tweet?

At the very least you should tweet four or five times per day. You want to stay active on Twitter in order to get more followers and to keep your current followers engaged. If you tweet five times per day that would mean you post four general information or humor tweets and one promotional tweet. If you follow these rules you can generate traffic from Twitter as part of your Internet marketing plan.

Email

Internet marketing constantly evolves. Some popular Internet marketing tools lose popularity and new ones emerge. Even the most enduring forms of Internet marketing change over time. A prime example is e-mail marketing.

Once the darling of online marketers, e-mail marketing became less popular as more people feared spam guards and blockers. However, e-mail marketing is a very powerful and viable form of Internet marketing.

The Basics

E-mail marketing is the best way to stay in contact with existing customers or potential customers. Your potential customer list should be people who specifically requested e-mails from you (do not buy e-mail lists).

The two key components to successful e-mail marketing are growing your list and staying in contact with your list.

Growing Your List

Growing your e-mail marketing list is essential. You do this is by offering people who visit your site something of value in exchange for their e-mail. There are a number of things you can consider, here are just a few:

• A coupon code or discount code

- Pre-sales event information

- A free trial offer

- A complimentary evaluation

- Free software or other downloadable files

- A whitepaper or report

It is also important to let people know that you will not sell their information or give it to anyone else. You should treat your e-mail list like gold because if you handle it properly it can be like gold.

Contacting Your List

It is important to stay in contact with your e-mail list. It is also important that you do not go overboard with that. If you overuse your e-mail database they will start to remove themselves from your distribution list.

The frequency you contact your e-mail list will depend on your business. For example, a real estate agent knows there is a window of opportunity to get a buyer. That window of opportunity may be only a couple of weeks so daily contact is appropriate. A clothes retailer has a much larger window of opportunity in fact the window never closes. Daily contact would be too much, weekly or bi-weekly contact is more appropriate.

Make sure your e-mails are different every time. Do not rehash the same information or promotions or you will turn off your e-mail list. If you keep these rules in mind, you can engage in effective e-mail marketing as part of your overall Internet marketing.

YouTube

Viral marketing is a goal for virtually all Internet marketing experts. Finding or creating the next big viral marketing video can be harder than finding a needle in a haystack. Your goal should not be trying to come up with the next YouTube sensation. Think smaller and you can succeed.

Consider having a YouTube contest!

The YouTube Contest

A YouTube Contest will enable you to harness the collective creativity of the contestants. If you offer a great prize and promote your contest well you should get a good number of entries.

The contest should be set up so that contestants submit their entries to your website (make sure they do NOT post them on YouTube). This will enable you to check the quality and appropriateness of an entry before it appears on YouTube.

The contest can be the creation of a 30-second commercial for your company or a product demonstration. Establish rules to protect your copyrights and brands and make sure it is clear that you own all rights to any videos submitted.

After reviewing all the entries choose the finalists (try for at least 10 finalists) and post the videos on your YouTube channel.

The Voting Equals Viral Marketing

Each finalist video will be on your YouTube channel, plus you should create a separate blog entry on your blog for each video. Voting is based on the number of views multiplied by the rating of the video on YouTube plus the number of social bookmarking votes on the blog (from Digg, StumbleUpon, etc.).

Basically you are setting up a voting system that will prompt the contestants to market their entry for you. They will send out the video link and ask that their contacts keep forwarding it off to their contact lists and so forth. This is creating 10 viral marketing campaigns or more depending on how many finalists you have.

Keep the voting period to about 60 days before announcing the winner.

The Results

The results need to be tabulated carefully. Once you have tabulated the votes you should announce the winner or winners and the prize they received.

A YouTube contest is an easy way to create multiple viral marketing opportunities based on the creativity of your contestants. Make sure you market the contest well to maximize the number of entries and the quality of them. This is a great system for Internet marketing you can consider.

Facebook

Internet marketing has changed dramatically as a result of social media websites like Facebook. This social media site is a force to be reckoned with as millions of people from around the world are on it at any given moment.

The very nature of Facebook makes it an Internet marketing jewel, especially for pay-per-click ads. With scores of information about every user the site can be used to pinpoint your audience for advertisements.

Internet Marketing with Specificity

Pay-per-click ads can be placed on many websites and search engines including Google, Yahoo and Bing. These search engines reach billions of people which make them powerful. The one thing that is lacking is the ability to place your ads only in front of your specific target market.

On Facebook you can be highly specific with targeting your ads. You can dictate who sees your ads based on criteria including:

• Age

• Gender

• Marital status

• Interests and hobbies

• Education level

• Geographic location

Your ability to place your ads only in front of a defined target market makes Facebook a great Internet marketing tool.

Know Your Market & Learn Your Market

The first step in placing effective Facebook ads would be to know your market. You should have a deep understanding of who your market is and who it is not. The more you know about your target market the more effective your Internet marketing will be.

You can use Facebook to learn about your target market. By identifying customers on Facebook you can start to see what interests them by the groups they join and participate in as well as the types of things they post.

Create your own Facebook group and invite people to participate in it. This is an invaluable way to learn about your target market.

Grow Your Facebook Fan Base

Grow your Facebook fan base by offering them incentives to join your group. You can offer discount codes and "inside information". If you give something of value people will become a friend and fan of yours on Facebook.

Using Facebook is a great way to reach your target market and learn about your target market. Take the time to create a good profile and fan page. Update your pages often and stay in communication with your fan base and you will reap the rewards of Facebook.

Help Customers Find You through SEO

Search engine optimization (SEO) is something we hear about often when researching Internet marketing. For someone new to Internet marketing, SEO may seem like just another acronym in a sea of acronyms. So, let us begin with the basics.

Search Engine Optimization Defined

Anytime you enter a search in Google, Yahoo, Bing or any other search engine, the search engine must determine which websites will appear in the results page. The way search engines do this is with a complicated mathematical formula that compares all the pages on the Internet against each other.

The comparison of web pages is done to determine which web pages are the most relevant for the search term you entered in. The factors that are considered in the formula include:

• The words in the URL

• The words used in the text

• The tags placed in the coding of the site

• The links from other sites that go to your sites

Search engine optimization is a series of tools and practices that enhance your site's score in the formula so your website appears in the search results.

Why SEO is Important

Search engines divide the search results on a webpage to include sponsored listings (pay-per-click ads) and natural listings. Most consumers know the difference between the sponsored listings and the natural listings.

Consumers generally equate a website's position in search results with the quality of the company. Though there is no real correlation between the two, the perception is an important one to be aware of.

SEO is also unlike pay-per-click because you do not have to pay every time someone clicks on your listing in the search results. Though you may hire someone to do your SEO campaign, their fee is the only cost associated with getting traffic through search engine optimization.

Pitfalls of SEO

It is important to know that SEO takes time to reap results. Unlike Pay-Per-Click ads that can bring traffic to your site in minutes, SEO generally takes several weeks to many months to bring traffic to your website.

Many website owners view SEO as an essential long-term marketing initiative rather than an immediate, instant traffic initiative like PPC or taking out ads on other websites.

If your goal is long-term success online your Internet marketing plan should include search engine optimization for your most important search terms.

Chapter 9- Money-Making Tactics for Business Success

1. Getting Past Fear of Failure

Being afraid of failure is a normal emotion for every person on the planet. How you get past that fear is the determining factor between failing and succeeding. You can do that by setting realistic goals and then examining those goals on occasion to do any necessary realignment. Above all, believe in yourself and the desire burning within that you can achieve it.

2. Make Opportunities

Rather than wait for money opportunity to find you, you need to find money opportunities. This might be watching for business opportunities in the paper regarding small businesses being sold, great real estate opportunities, and investments with stocks, bonds, or mutual funds, taking a talent and turning it into an entrepreneurial adventure. People that have reached financial status will tell you that they look for ways to seize opportunities, not wait for opportunities to come knocking on their door because it will not happen that way.

3. Make the Best of Each Day

Try to live every day as though it were your last. Make the most of every day and accomplish something. Even if it is something small, every baby step adds up to a huge success in the end.

4. Have a Plan

Even if it is flimsy to begin with, you should construct a plan to include goal, milestones, deliverables such as contracts, business plans, etc., and accomplishments. This will provide you with a visual as to what you are working for, what milestones you have successfully met, and where you need to do better.

5. Seek Input

Whatever your idea of to make money, conduct a "sanity check" throughout the process of reaching your goal. This should be done with someone you trust and who is themselves successful. Ask them to provide honest feedback about your success and as you move through different milestones, bounce concerns or new ideas off them to help keep you on the right track.

6. Stay Motivated

When striving for the big goal of success to make more money in life, it is critical to stay motivated. Find inspiring and motivational tapes, seminars, books, movies; whatever you are able to get your hands on. When you start to feel a little down and out and doubt starts to creep in, turn to these motivational tools to help you keep on track. A few excellent motivators include Tony Robbins, Norman Vincent Peale, Jim Rohn, Zig Ziglar, and Les Brown.

7. Don't Settle

If you have a goal of making one million dollar and you know you have both desire and skill, do not just settle to make one hundred thousand only. While that may be good training ground, do not allow yourself to lose sight of your ultimate goal.

8. No Excuses

Many famous actors, music artists, inventors, etc., had special challenges ranging from learning disabilities to physical disabilities. Take Beethoven for example. He was born deaf yet he went on to be one of the world's greatest composers or Joni Erickson who was paralyzed from the neck down yet she learned to paint with her mouth. Today, her paintings are famous around the world and worth millions. If you are faced with a special challenge of your own when you are trying to make more money, while you may have to adjust things from time to time, do not use excuses. If you want something bad enough, there is a way!

9. Patience and Dues

Succeeding to make more money takes time. A goal worth setting will take time to achieve. Be patient with yourself, the people around you, and the process it takes to become successful, also referred to as "paying your dues." Pay your dues by learning and working your way up the ladder to success.

10. Be Thankful

You need to be thankful for not only your accomplishments but also your failures. Having a grateful attitude is important. It will help you stay humble, which in turn, will help you continue striving for the ultimate in success.

11. Focus on What You Like

To increase your chance of succeeding to make money, you should concentrate your efforts on something you enjoy. When you start out, make a list of everything you find interesting. Then in a second column, write down the skills you have in relation to each of those items. This will help you narrow choices down based on interest and skill, which gets you started in the right direction for success in making money.

12. Keep a Journal

As you work hard to become financially rich, you need to be able to see your accomplishments. Start a journal and track everything you have conquered. When you feel discouraged or frustrated, reflect on what you have achieved, and rejuvenate yourself.

13. Rewards

When children do something great, parents will reward them with something nice, whether a kind word of encouragement or a new toy. When people do well in their job, they get raises. As you surpass your milestones, reward yourself. Treat yourself to something nice – a new dress, a new fishing pole, whatever you like, be sure to award yourself for a job well done.

14. Watch for Scams

Whether you are just starting out or expanding an existing business, unfortunately, there are thousands of people waiting to defraud you out of money. If something appears too good to be true – IT IS! Always conduct thorough research and never jump into opportunities that look perfect. If someone becomes pushy, wanting you to make a quick decision on any type of investment, do not walk away – RUN away!

15. Don't Neglect Things

Especially when things are small and do not appear to have a major impact on the big picture, you need to ensure you follow through and complete your tasks. Those little things can quickly add up to a big mess if not taken care of in a timely and efficient manner.

16. Associate and Collaborate with Others

More than likely, you will reach various times when you do not have the appropriate expertise to make more money. This is the time collaboration and/or networking is valuable. These relationships can help you answer questions, provide guidance, and provide the ongoing support and encouragement you will need.

17. Repositioning and Reflection

On occasion, reflect on what you have accomplished as well as your open milestones and ensure you are still heading in the right direction. Repositioning along the way to success is perfectly normal and to be expected. You may have been struggling with something specific. Rather than continue battling this issue, reflect on what has not been working, and reposition yourself so you do not have to keep battling the same things repeatedly.

18. Get out of Debt

Take time to get any debts paid off, especially credit card debts that will cost you a fortune in interest. This is especially important if you will be seeking funding to make more money. You want to ensure that your records and credit are clean if you need to make a presentation before an investor, asking for money.

19. Continue To Read

Stay current on the industry news that your goal falls in. Learn about current trends, company failures or successes, new ideas; whatever information you can find. For example, if you have decided to open a retail store and have a great idea and a real passion for your goal, read about that specific type of store, location, potential revenue, downfalls, everything. This information will be a part of your business plan and is crucial.

20. Take Notes

How many times have you had an idea on how to make more money either through a dream, while doing the dishes, or sitting at your desk, and have thought that as soon as you have time, you will make a note of it. When that free time rolls around, you have forgotten some or all of that great money-making idea. Keep a journal or notepad handy at all times. When you have an idea, write it down immediately.

21. Take Care of Yourself

Being financially rich means taking care of you, both physically and emotionally. You will need to have energy, focus, and rest. In turn, this will help you concentrate and put in the hours required to be successful. Without taking proper care of yourself, you will end up struggling and your business could feel the effects.

22. Be Serious

Take your efforts to make more money seriously. Making money is a serious thing and it takes serious dedication. You have to have the mindset that this is not going to be all play, at least not in the beginning.

23. Apply What You Learn

Since you will be setting milestones as you reach for your success to make more money, apply what you have learned through each phase of the process. Doing is a much more powerful tool than simply reading or watching.

24. Avoid Stress

When you strive to be financially successful, stress is a natural part of the process. Do everything you can to avoid stress. Adding in unnecessary stress into the equation will take focus away from accomplishing your goals. You can listen to relaxing tapes, get a professional massage, take a walk, or whatever helps you to relax. When you start feeling overwhelmed, stop, change direction, and avoid stress. The only thing stress accomplishes is draining your think power and creativity.

25. Learn How to Delegate

As you start getting closer to your goal of making more money, you will find that there are many more things to do than hours in the day. If going into business, consider hiring someone; even part-time or on a freelance basis to help take some of your load. You will be amazed at how much this will help ease the situation and allow you the proper amount of time to focus on the things that need your full attention.

26. Be a Problem Solver

Rather than stew over things or let stress overtake you, find ways to become a problem solver. Look at ways that you might find new customers, increase productivity, or resolve issues.

27. Conduct Research

It is important to know what you are getting into. First, you will want to conduct research as far as the business, industry, or interest associated with your particular success of making more money. Second, the research will help you stay up to date on trends, which may or may not require you to make adjustments in your own goal. For example, if you were interested in opening a particular business focusing on a specific technology and that technology took a turn to another direction, new advancements, you may need to change the direction you were going for your own business. Unless you kept up on research, you would not know when a change was needed and therefore, would end up building a business already headed for failure.

28. Be a Strong Leader

Learn to be a good leader and a good mentor. Enjoy making a difference and in guiding others to achieve their potential as well. Help people reach to new horizons.

29. Be Logical

Okay, you may be thinking that logic itself is logical. However, being logic in many cases means having some level of analytical ability. Regardless of the way you think, find the logic in it. This will help you think and plan clearly and honestly.

30. Raise your Standards

You may think you are working your tail off and you probably are. Try raising the bar just a little bit. Always expect the best from yourself. Do not beat yourself up if you do not always hit 100% but increase your standards and strive for more. Learn to 'Step Up'!

31. Unconscious Power

The unconscious mind is a very powerful tool. Take advantage of this and each night before heading off to bed, take some time to pose questions to yourself and then allow your mind to hash them out while you sleep. In addition, mediate in whatever way you find relaxing before going to bed to clear your mind from clutter and allow the subconscious mind to go to work.

32. Identify Procrastinations

If you have a problem with procrastination, make a list of the things you constantly put on hold. This will help you identify your poor patterns and make the appropriate adjustments. Local colleges often have improvement courses regarding making better decisions and procrastination. Locate a class that would help you with this kind of challenge.

33. Want versus Need

Strive for success because you want it, and not because you need it. When you want something, it brings about intention, desire, and action. However, when you need something, it will lead to pain, stress, and frustration.

34. Appreciate Life

Appreciate life, people, everything around you. Learn as much as you can from every person you meet. Do not turn people away just because you do not agree with them. You never know, the very people you turn away may be the very people that come to your life to being more money to you.

35. The Right Marketing

When you get ready to start marketing your business or idea, never rely on one method of marketing. It is important to look at several options since nothing will last forever.

36. Believe

Not only do you need to believe in the product or service you are building that will help you to attract more money, you also need to believe in you. Your confidence is what will get you through the difficult challenges and build credibility with your customers.

37. Guard your Emotions

Keeping emotions in check is not always an easy task. You will have times of disappointment that will require you to react with integrity. You may feel like crying and feel as though your world has just ended. Keep telling yourself that it has not ended and you will just have to make some adjustments in your plan. Never allow anger to be a response. You never know the trickle-down effect of that anger and how it could permanently damage your reputation.

38. Break Bad Habits

Habits, regardless of size or nature, can be exceptionally difficult to break. This will take a lot of effort but you can do it. Unfortunately, poor habits can be the one aspect of your behavior that could be the obstacle to making money. If you have a habit of sniffling or chewing your nails when you get nervous or saying demeaning or offensive things as a way of trying to control, to be successful, whether on a personal or business level, you have to stop.

39. Have Balance in your Life

You have to find balance not only for yourself but also for others around you. Balance means providing time away from work for pleasure, working extra hours when required, knowing when a new direction is required, etc. when you are striving to make more money.

ABOUT THE AUTHOR

Sandra Rodriguez didn't grow up wanting to be an entrepreneur. She wanted to be a preschool teacher because she has always loved teaching and young children. However, her first few years fulfilling "her dream" were riddled with challenges because of the lack of financial support her school was getting. She figured that her dream would entail raising enough funds to support the school and to provide the children with the quality education that they deserve.

This realization became the turning point of her career.

Sandra worked hard to learn everything that needs to learn when starting a business. She began doing affiliate marketing until she had enough capital to start her own business.

Today, Sandra is a volunteer teacher and an active patron of the local preschool. She is a mother to Theodore and Nathan and a loving wife to husband, Marc.